NATURAL WORLD

GREAT WHITE
SHARK

HABITATS • LIFE CYCLES • FOOD CHAINS • THREATS

Brett Westwood

WAYLAND

WWF

Produced in Association with WWF-UK

NATURAL WORLD

Chimpanzee • Crocodile • Dolphin • Elephant • Giant Panda
Great White Shark • Killer Whale • Lion • Orangutan
Penguin • Polar Bear • Tiger

Produced for Wayland Publishers Ltd by
Roger Coote Publishing
Gissing's Farm, Fressingfield
Suffolk IP21 5SH

First published in 1999 by
Wayland Publishers Limited
61 Western Road, Hove
East Sussex BN3 1JD, England

All Wayland books encourage children to read and help them improve their literacy.

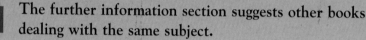

✓ The contents page, page numbers, headings and index help locate specific pieces of information.

✓ The glossary reinforces alphabetic knowledge and extends vocabulary.

✓ The further information section suggests other books dealing with the same subject.

Find Wayland on the Internet at http://www.wayland.co.uk

Cover: Face to face with the great white shark.
Title page: A great white surfaces, jaws agape.
Contents page: Underside view of the great white.
Index page: A great white moves sleekly through the water.

WWF is a registered charity no. 201707
WWF-UK, Panda House, Weyside Park
Godalming, Surrey GU7 1XR

British Library Cataloguing in Publication Data
Westwood, Brett
  Great white shark: habitats, life cycles, food chains, threats. - (Natural world)
  1.White shark - Juvenile literature
  I.Title
  597.3'3

Picture acknowledgements
Bruce Coleman Collection 11 (Carl Roessler), 24 (Christer Fredriksson), 32 (Carl Roessler), 33 (Jeffrey Rotman), 37 (Pacific Stock); Digital Stock/Marty Snyderman 3, 6, 7, 10, 13, 15, 16, 17, 18, 22, 36, 38, 44 middle, 44 bottom, 48; Planet Earth Pictures *front cover* (James D Watt), 8, (James D Watt), 9 (Doug Perrine), 12 (Doug Perrine), 14 (Peter Scoones), 20 (James D Watt), 23 (Peter Scoones), 25 (Rodney Fox), 27 (Herwarth Voigtmann), 28 (Douglas David Seifert), 29 (Flip Schulke), 34 (Carl Roessler), 35 (Douglas David Seifert), 39 (Peter Scoones), 40 (Alex Kerstitch), 42 (Doug Perrine), 43 (Carl Roessler), 44 top (Doug Perrine), 45 middle (Carl Roessler), 45 bottom (Peter Scoones); Still Pictures 30 (Jeffrey Rotman), 31 (Jeffrey Rotman), 41 (Jeffrey Rotman); Stock Market 1, 26, 45 top. All artwork by Michael Posen except page 21 by Peter Bull.

ISBN 0 7502 2452 5

Printed and bound by G. Canale & C. S.p.A., Turin, Italy

Contents

Meet the Great White

The great white shark is one of the most powerful hunters in the world's oceans. This huge fish is feared by people more than any other creature. It has rows of sharp teeth for slicing through flesh and will eat seals, penguins and dolphins. But it is also one of the planet's most mysterious animals, as we know very little about how it lives, breeds and dies.

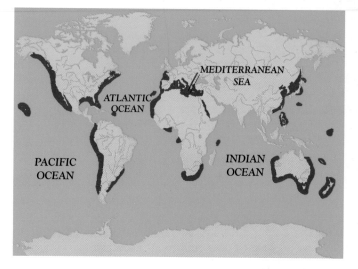

▲ The red shading on this map shows where great white sharks live.

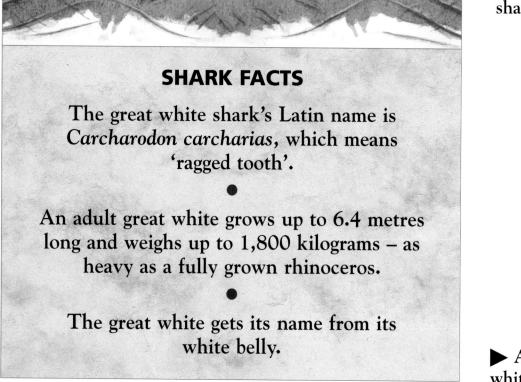

SHARK FACTS

The great white shark's Latin name is *Carcharodon carcharias*, which means 'ragged tooth'.

●

An adult great white grows up to 6.4 metres long and weighs up to 1,800 kilograms – as heavy as a fully grown rhinoceros.

●

The great white gets its name from its white belly.

▶ An adult male great white shark.

Sensitive pits
On the underside of the shark's snout are tiny pits, called ampullae of Lorenzini. The pits are filled with jelly and can detect weak electrical currents in the water.

Gills
Slits called gills allow oxygen from the water to pass into the shark's bloodstream.

Dorsal fin
This triangular fin on the shark's back prevents the shark from rolling over in the water and helps it balance in rough seas.

Eyes
The shark's black eyes cannot blink, but they can be rolled back in their sockets for protection. They have a special reflective layer, called a tapetum, to help the shark see in the murky depths.

Teeth
A great white has about 200 teeth at any one time. Some of them have saw-like edges for biting big chunks from prey.

Skin
The shark's skin is rough like sandpaper, and covered with tiny tooth-like scales called denticles.

Pectoral fins
Two pectoral fins, one on either side, help to keep the shark's body stable in the water.

Claspers
The male has special fins called claspers, which it uses when mating.

Lateral line
The great white shark has a line of special pits and nerves along its side that are sensitive to changes in water pressure. This enables the shark to detect underwater sounds and movement.

Tail
The shark flicks its powerful forked tail to gain extra speed when chasing fish.

The Great White and its Relatives

The great white shark is the largest flesh-eating member of the shark family. There are about 350 species of shark, found in all the world's oceans, from tropical coral reefs to the icy waters of the Arctic.

The shark family includes the world's largest fish – the enormous whale shark, which can grow to 13 metres long. The whale shark feeds entirely on plankton and is harmless to humans. Skates and rays are also related to sharks.

▼ Whitetip reef sharks are members of a shark family called requiem sharks. They often swim in small groups around coral reefs.

Great whites belong to a group of sharks known as the mackerel sharks. They all have long snouts and large teeth for feeding on fast-swimming fish such as mackerel and tuna. Like its relatives, the great white shark lives quite close to the shore (see the map on page 4). It may occasionally travel out into the open ocean.

▲ The southern stingray, like all rays, has flattened wings to help it 'fly' through the water. Its whip-like tail contains a poisonous spine. You can see how big the stingray is compared to the diver in the photo behind it.

An Awesome Ancestor

The largest adult great white sharks ever recorded were about 7 metres long. A great white as big as this is a very impressive fish, but its ancestors were even bigger.

The first sharks appeared in the seas 350 million years ago. By 50 million years ago they had evolved into the biggest flesh-eating fish ever to have lived on the planet. A giant shark called Megalodon had teeth larger than a man's hand and grew to a length of more than 15 metres.

▲ Imagine a shark twice the size of the great white and you get an idea of why the great white's massive ancestor Megalodon was feared by even the biggest whales millions of years ago.

▼ A fossilized Megalodon tooth dwarfs the tooth of a great white shark. Megalodon's teeth were black or brown. Fossilized Megalodon teeth have been found in deserts, proving that the land once lay under ancient seas.

Megalodon's fossilized teeth are the only parts of it that survive today, but their shape and size make scientists believe that Megalodon was similar to the modern great white shark.

Megalodon's jaws were so big that a person could stand upright in them. We cannot be sure what it caught with them, but whale remains have been found along with the shark's teeth, so it is possible the world's largest fish once fed on the world's largest mammal.

Skeleton and Movement

The great white is perfectly at home in its underwater world. Its skeleton has no bones, but is made of an elastic substance called cartilage, which is light and allows the shark to move quickly and gracefully through the water.

Movement is very important to the great white. It pushes itself through the water by moving its sleek, muscular body from side to side, aided by flicks of its forked tail.

▲ With its streamlined body shape, the great white cuts through the water with ease. Its tail and body have evolved to allow it to cruise slowly, but also move in bursts of speed to catch fast-moving prey such as tuna.

Breathing

Like all fish, the great white breathes through its gills. Water is forced through the gill slits as the shark moves forwards. The gills' lining absorbs oxygen from the water. The great white has no muscles to push water through the gills, so it has to keep moving at all times: if it stops swimming it will die from a lack of oxygen.

▼ The shark has five gill-openings in front of its pectoral fins.

A Shark is Born

Young sharks are called pups. They hatch from eggs while inside their mother's womb and grow there for several months until they are born. No one has ever seen a female great white shark giving birth.

Sometimes the pups eat their first meal before they are born, by feeding on unhatched eggs in the womb. The eggs are provided by the mother so that when the sharks are born, they have had plenty of nourishment to keep them going while they learn how to hunt.

▲ Like this lemon shark, the great white shark chooses a quiet spot in which to give birth. She looks for a place where there are few currents and no other sharks, who might eat her new-born babies.

As soon as it is born, the shark pup quickly explores its new world, and the creatures it shares it with. Strong currents may carry the pup far off into the ocean, so it cruises in shallow water close to caves and reefs. If the water is too cold, the shark can keep warm by raising its body temperature by up to ten degrees higher than the surrounding water.

As it swims, the pup may meet a green turtle paddling along with its scaly flippers or even an inquisitive sea lion. They are too big to be eaten... yet!

SHARK PUPS

A female great white shark normally gives birth to as many as 10 pups, though she can carry up to 15 embryos (unborn babies). The new-born pups are about 120 centimetres long, and they weigh about 16 kilograms – as much as a two-year-old child.

▼ This green turtle's tough shell and scaly flippers protect it from the teeth of a great white pup. Younger turtles have softer shells and make an ideal snack.

Fending for Itself

The new-born shark pup has to look after itself and receives no help from its parents. Its father may have left the area and its mother will be busy feeding to build up her strength after giving birth.

Food and safety are very important to the shark pup. One of the main dangers it faces is being eaten by adult great whites and other sharks. Its keen eyesight and sense of smell will protect it in its mysterious new world.

▼ The new-born pup instinctively knows how to swim and where to find food, and is led by its nose and keen eyesight to explore its new home.

▲ With a mouthful of razor-sharp teeth, the barracuda (centre) could be a danger to the young great white pup if it swims too far into open water.

The shark pup is a perfectly formed miniature version of its parents, and is born with the same hunting skills. Its teeth are slimmer than those of the adult sharks. This is because it eats mainly small fishes, which are slippery and would be harder to hold with broader teeth.

The great white pup will try other food, including crabs, shrimps and small lobsters. As it tries out different foods, it will sometimes make mistakes. Glass bottles, tin cans and even a straw hat have been found in the stomachs of great white sharks!

Learning to Hunt

For the first few months of its life, the shark pup practices swimming and catching food. Its eyes are adapted to seeing in clear water near the surface, but it can also detect prey that is out of sight using the sensitive pits on its snout and its lateral line (see page 5).

▲ A shark's eyes work well in sunlit water and the pup soon learns to hunt shoals of fish just below the surface of the sea.

With flicks of its strong tail, the pup chases shoals of fish and squid at speeds of up to 30 kilometres per hour. Like all sharks, it feeds mainly on moving prey and will often single out the weakest and slowest fish in a shoal.

Not all fish are good to eat. Great whites in the Red Sea soon learn to avoid the brightly coloured lionfish, which has poison-tipped spines that can pierce their soft undersides.

The pups also steer clear of another Red Sea fish, the Moses sole. When attacked, this bottom-dwelling flatfish produces a slime that paralyzes the young shark's jaws, so that the fish can escape.

▼ The candy-striped lionfish lives on coral reefs and is hard to miss because of its long, ribbon-like fins. It swims fearlessly in open water because it is protected by poisonous spines.

A great white pup grows very fast. By the end of its first year, it will be 30 centimetres longer than when it was born, and it will continue to grow at this rate for the next 15 years.

▼ These Atlantic spotted dolphins swim together to avoid shark attacks. An adult great white is more likely to attack a lone dolphin, or one that is sick or dying, than several dolphins in a group.

As the shark grows, it eats bigger and bigger prey. It still catches squid and fish, including other sharks, but it also begins to prey on mammals, including seals, sea lions, porpoises and dolphins. Some dolphins have bite scars and ragged fins that show they have had a close encounter with a shark.

GREAT WHITE SHARK FOOD CHAIN

Great white shark

Small shark

Seal

Penguin

Fish

Animal plankton

Plant plankton

Great whites also eat birds. When young shearwaters or other seabirds are ready to leave the nest, the sharks gather offshore and wait for the clumsy young birds to take their first flight. As they settle on the sea to rest, the sharks grab them from beneath and swallow them whole.

Great white sharks sometimes eat dead animals. Often, several sharks will gather around a dead whale and share in this vast meal. Great whites have huge appetites. They may eat so much in a single meal that they can go for many days, even weeks, without feeding.

▲ At the bottom of the great white shark's food chain are tiny plants and animals called plankton. Most fish feed on plankton, which swarm in the oceans in their billions.

▲ A close-up view of the shark's head shows the small pits on its snout, which can detect tiny electric currents in the water. This shark has scars over its eye and on its nose, probably from fighting with other great whites.

Shark Senses

Like adult great whites, the shark pup has an amazing sense of smell, and can detect the scent of blood in the sea up to half a kilometre away. But smell is only one of the senses it uses to find its prey.

Tiny hairs along the shark's lateral line detect changes in the water pressure and send messages to its brain. From these messages, the shark can tell if there is a shoal of fish nearby.

It can also see reasonably well in murky water, because it has a special layer called a tapetum at the back of its eyes. The tapetum acts as a mirror and reflects as much light as possible into the eyes.

When animals move in the water, they produce very small electric currents as their hearts beat or their fins vibrate. The great white can locate its prey by detecting this electricity using the sensitive pits on its snout.

▼ This diagram shows the different senses a shark uses to detect prey. A shark can hear sounds at least 1,000 metres away. As it gets closer, the shark's keen sense of smell guides it towards its prey, while its other senses help it move in for the kill.

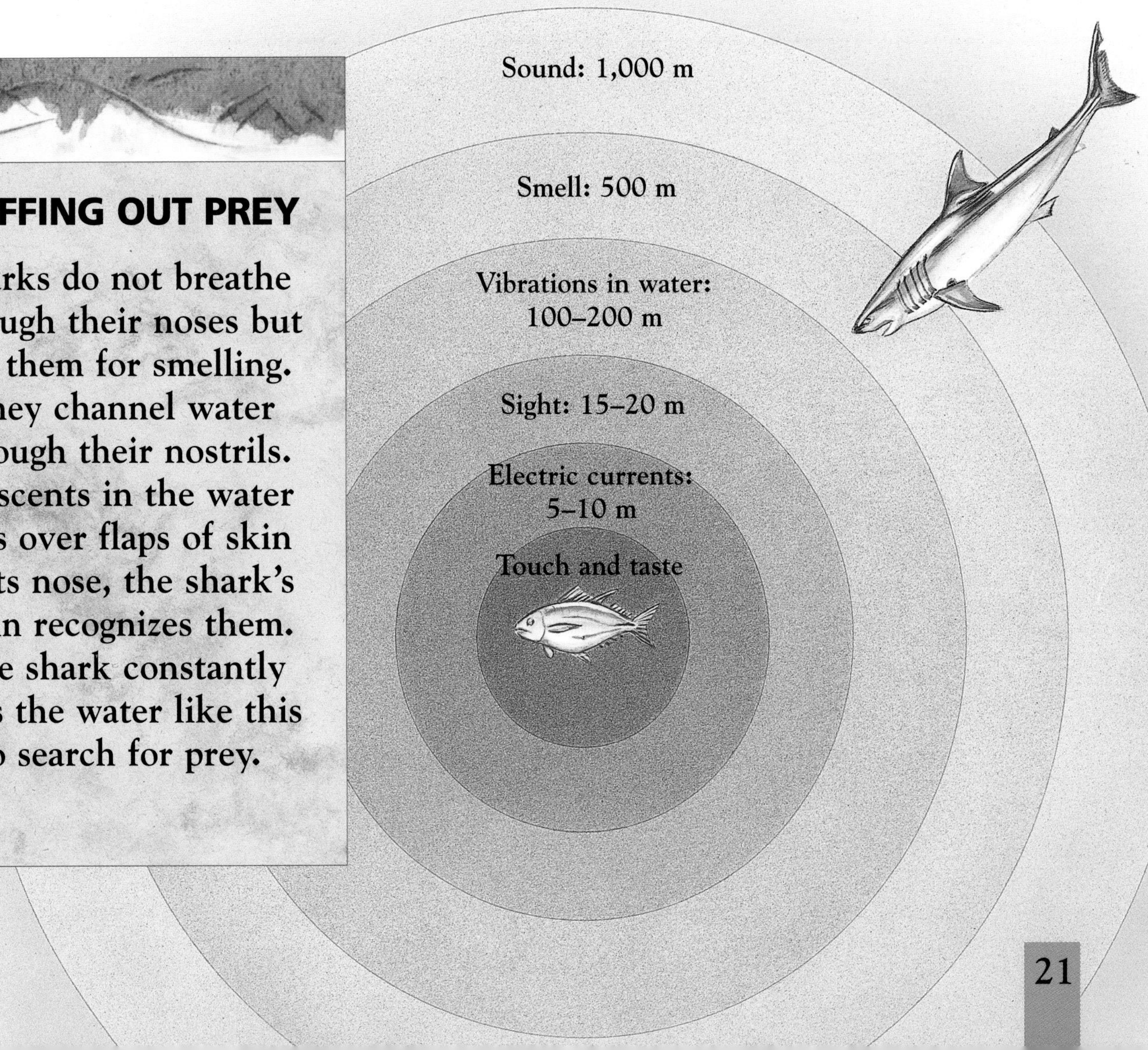

SNIFFING OUT PREY

Sharks do not breathe through their noses but use them for smelling. They channel water through their nostrils. As scents in the water pass over flaps of skin in its nose, the shark's brain recognizes them. The shark constantly tests the water like this to search for prey.

Sound: 1,000 m

Smell: 500 m

Vibrations in water: 100–200 m

Sight: 15–20 m

Electric currents: 5–10 m

Touch and taste

Camouflage

A hunting shark takes its prey by surprise. Guided by a mixture of electrical signals, smells and changes in water pressure, the shark swims closer until its victim is in sight.

The shark's colouring acts as camouflage in the water and allows it to move in for the kill without being spotted by its prey. When seen from above, the shark's grey back helps it blend in with the ocean depths. Viewed from below, the shark's white belly hides it against the pale surface waters. This pattern of light and dark is called counter-shading.

▼ A shark turns in the water, showing its white belly and dark grey back.

▲ This fur seal is hunting for food in shallow water. In open, deeper water, its dark shape near the surface would make it an obvious target for sharks swimming underneath.

Sharks feeding on penguins, seals and dolphins approach from below, so that their prey shows up as a dark shape against the lighter water near the surface. Then they rush upwards with such force that the prey is sometimes catapulted out of the water.

Great whites are the only fish that search for prey by sticking their heads out of the water. In South Africa, they wait offshore and look for seals on the rocks.

Shark-watching

One of the best places in the world to watch great white sharks hunting is just off the coast of the South Africa's Western Cape. Here, sharks swim up and down the narrow channel between Dyer Island and Geyser Rock searching for Cape fur seals.

About 60,000 fur seals live on Geyser Rock, attracted by the shoals of fish just offshore. Dyer Island is also home to 20,000 jackass penguins.

▼ The South African jackass penguin brays like a donkey and breeds in huge colonies on rocky islands near the coast. Great white sharks wait offshore to feed on adults and young chicks.

24

Sometimes the sharks leap out of the water as they chase their seal victims through the 600-metre channel, known to local people as 'Shark Alley'. Although great white sharks normally hunt alone, several will stalk seals in 'Shark Alley' at the same time, and fights over food occasionally break out between them.

Injured seals missing large chunks of flesh sometimes escape the sharks and haul themselves onto Hospital Rock in the middle of the channel. The lucky ones will rest here before returning to Geyser Rock, though some will die from their injuries.

▲ This seal has been bitten by a shark. In spite of its injury, it has managed to scramble on to the rocks. If it is lucky, its wounds will heal.

Shark Bite!

When a great white shark moves in for the kill, it speeds straight towards its prey, lifting its nose and dropping its lower jaw to increase the size of its mouth. The last view of a great white that the victim gets is of rows of gleaming white teeth as the shark prepares to bite.

The shark tears away a huge chunk of flesh. As it strikes, the shark rolls its eyes back in their sockets, to protect them in case the prey struggles.

▲ An attacking shark sometimes rears out of the water as it tries to reach its prey. This fearsome sight has thrilled shark watchers for generations.

FOOD FIGHTS

If two great whites meet over a kill, one may twist its body and slap its tail on the water's surface to try and scare off the other. If the intruder's tail-slaps are stronger or more frequent than its rival's, it will be allowed to share the meal.

If the prey is not killed instantly, the shark backs off and waits for it to bleed to death before carrying on eating. Great whites will not risk being injured by animals thrashing around in the water. Some fish, seabirds and seal pups are swallowed whole.

▼ Some sharks, such as this member of the mackerel shark family, cover their eyes with a special eyelid when they feed. Great whites roll their eyes back into their sockets to protect them.

Teeth and Jaws

What makes a shark bite so terrible are its powerful jaws and triangular teeth, which are as hard as steel. The shark has several rows of teeth and if it loses one from its front row, another tooth slides forward from behind to take its place. During its life, the shark may lose and replace up to 40,000 teeth. Some sharks replace a tooth every eight days.

▼ Just before attacking, a shark opens its mouth wide and its teeth move outwards and forwards.

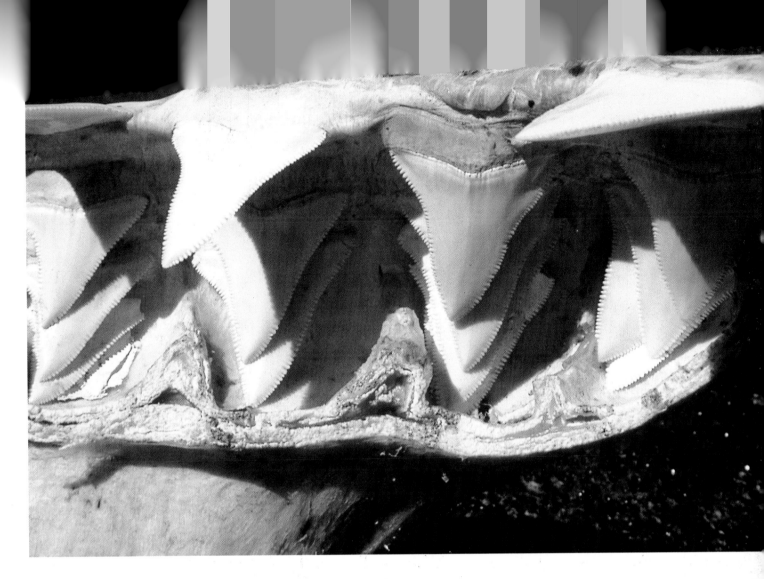

▲ This pair of shark jaw bones clearly shows the rows of sharp teeth. The teeth near the back are longer and sharper and will move forward as the front ones wear out.

Each tooth ends in a razor-sharp point and its saw-like edges are ideal for cutting through flesh or seal-blubber. When the shark bites, the teeth in its lower jaw pin the prey so that the upper teeth can cut through the flesh.

Because the shark's skeleton is made of elastic cartilage, not bones, the only part of its body that survives after it dies are its teeth. Fossilized shark teeth from millions of years ago tell scientists about the types of shark that hunted in the prehistoric oceans.

▲ In places where sharks are known to appear close to the shore, signs like this warn bathers of the danger.

Danger – Shark!

Stories in films, books, magazines and newspapers have given the great white shark a fearsome reputation. Although it feeds close to the shore – often near beaches – and sometimes does kill people, most shark attacks are accidental and humans are certainly not its favourite food.

HOW MUCH DANGER?

There are probably no more than 10 attacks by great white sharks around the world in any one year and most of these are not fatal. The areas with the most risk of attack are California, South Africa and Southern Australia, though there is even one record of an attack off Italy.

Great whites occasionally attack divers and surfers in wetsuits because the shark mistakes the rubber wetsuit for the shiny skin of a seal or dolphin. Surfboards look rather like huge fish from below, which is why sharks will bite chunks from them. Spear-fishers are also more likely to be bitten because they carry bleeding fish, which attract the sharks' attention.

When a shark attacks a human, it rarely eats its victim. When a great white bites a person, it is probably doing a simple 'taste test' to see if the person is worth eating.

▼ A diver holds up photos of his injuries after he was attacked by a great white shark (left) and after he was stitched up (right). Despite these terrible injuries, he soon recovered and returned to study sharks!

Adult Life

As the great white shark grows older, it gets heavier and stronger. As it hunts for food, the great white's skin becomes scarred by the bites it receives from its prey. Scientists studying great whites have learned to recognize individuals from the patterns of scars on their skin.

▼ The shark has now grown into a 5-metre-long fish, one of the fiercest hunters in the sea.

SHARK SKIN

In the past, the great white's tough, dried skin, known as shagreen, was used for polishing wood. Shark skin is still used in some parts of the world for making hard-wearing shoes.

Adult great whites are sometimes bitten by the sea lions or dolphins they try to catch. Others are scarred by wounds they receive from spear-fishers, or if they get caught in nets.

Sharks also bite each other. Sometimes divers attract great whites with lumps of meat or tuna. The adults and young compete for food, and the bigger sharks occasionally attack the smaller ones, leaving them scarred forever.

▲ Divers watch a great white shark underwater from the safety of a metal cage. Even with the protection of the cage, the sight of those dark eyes and huge teeth can be frightening.

Mating

Female great white sharks can give birth to their first pups at about 12 years old. No-one has ever photographed great whites mating, but their courtship is probably similar to the behaviour of other mackerel sharks. Mating probably takes place at night.

Once a male great white has found a female, he swims close to her and gently bites her fins and belly. Biting helps to put the female in the mood for mating. Before the mating season begins, her skin grows thicker to cope with this rough treatment, but she is left with scars and ragged fins as a result of the courtship.

▲ When a male is ready to mate, he searches for a female. The male mates with his clasper fins, which can be seen between his pectoral fins and his tail.

▶ Scientists can identify individual sharks by the wavy pattern on their sides. They don't yet know whether sharks use the same method to tell each other apart.

The male mates using his specially shaped clasper fins, which are as long as a cricket or baseball bat. The male rolls the claspers into a tube-shape and puts them into the female's body. Most sharks mate belly to belly. As the male shark gets older, his claspers increase in length.

The young sharks are born several months – perhaps up to a year – after mating has taken place.

Lifespan of the Great White

A great white shark can expect to live for about 30 years, but many probably do not survive this long. Because great white sharks are at the top of the food chain (see page 17) they have no natural predators in the world's oceans.

A great white's real enemies are surprisingly small. As it gets older, its body becomes home to parasitic worms and leeches, which suck its blood and rob it of its food supply. Thousands of tapeworms have been found in the intestines of a single shark. When it grows weak, it can also be attacked by fungi, which rot its skin and eventually kill it.

▶ A head-on view of an old great white shark. As it grows older, the shark's teeth become longer, while the denticles on its skin grow longer and also broader with age.

▼ The only sea-hunter larger than the great white is the orca, or killer whale. An orca was once seen attacking an adult great white, but sharks are not its normal prey.

Threats

In spite of its size and strength, the great white does have one enemy that could wipe it out forever – humans. No one knows how many great white sharks there are in the seas, but we do know that many are killed by humans each year, either by accident or on purpose. Large numbers are hooked or speared by trophy fishers, who kill the sharks for sport and for their jaws, which are sold to tourists.

▼ Fishing for shark trophies is still legal in most places where the great whites live. Sports fishers try to catch the largest sharks, which are often breeding females.

Some sharks may die out or move away from an area if their main food source disappears. In California, elephant seals were nearly wiped out in the 1970s, when people hunted them for their meat and blubber. Great white sharks left the area, but came back when the hunting stopped and the numbers of elephant seals increased again.

▲ These northern elephant seals live on the Farallon Islands off the coast of California. They are an important source of food for local great white sharks.

Many great white sharks drown when they become trapped in the nets used to catch tuna. We don't know how many sharks die in this way, because their bodies are thrown away at sea. It is likely to be several thousand, because each net is several kilometres long. Great whites also die in the nets used to protect swimmers on some beaches.

Other sharks are caught for their body-meat or for the natural oils they contain, which are a source of Vitamin A. Shark's teeth are turned into brooches or necklaces and sold around the world. In North Africa, shark skin is polished and used as leather.

Many sharks give birth in shallow water, such as in mangrove swamps or quiet bays. Building development in these areas may destroy the natural environment and threaten the sharks' existence.

▶ A great white shark caught off Sicily in the Mediterranean Sea. Some of the largest great whites have been caught in the Mediterranean.

▼ Many species of shark are in danger. Thousands of tonnes of dried fins from millions of sharks are cooked and turned into shark-fin soup in China and some other Asian countries.

The future

Protecting great white sharks is difficult, because so little is known about them. Until we know where they breed, how often they give birth and how far they travel, it is hard to conserve their numbers. The idea of protecting such a large, dangerous hunter was once thought of as foolish. Today, however, many people realise that the great white shark could be in danger of extinction from fishing and threats to its habitat.

▲ These researchers are using a machine called a hydrophone to track the movements of a great white shark. The hydrophone detects sound signals sent out by a tiny transmitter inserted under the shark's skin.

Already some countries have banned deliberate fishing for great white sharks. South Africa was the first country to do this in 1991 and Namibia followed two years later. In the US state of California, it is also illegal to catch and kill them for sport. An International Shark Plan is now being put together to help countries learn about their sharks and to control how many are caught.

▼ The great white shark is one of the finest hunters the world has ever seen. Scientists are only just beginning to learn the truth about the life of this beautiful, powerful fish.

As scientists continue to study the great white shark and discover more about it, we will hopefully learn how to save this amazing creature. Some of the organizations involved in helping the great white shark are listed on page 47.

Great White Life Cycle

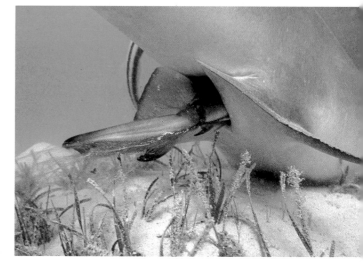

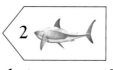 A mother shark gives birth to up to 15 shark pups, each one about 120 centimetres long. Some unlucky sharks are eaten by their brothers and sisters before they are born. Their mother leaves them to fend for themselves.

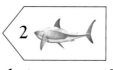 The young shark pups look like smaller versions of their parents. They can hunt for fish and crabs as soon as they are born. Their teeth are very sharp and pointed for catching small fish.

 After a year, the shark pup has grown by about another 30 centimetres. It swims alone and practises chasing shoals of fish by using its strong, forked tail.

 **4** By the time it is four or five years old, the shark has grown fatter and much longer. Now it hunts bigger prey such as tuna and young sea lions. It stalks its victims, camouflaged by the pattern of colours on its skin.

5 At about twelve years old, the shark is now an adult. The males have grown long claspers, which they use to mate with the females. During mating the males nibble their partner's fins and bodies, leaving scars for life.

6 The fully-grown adult shark is an excellent hunter. It has learned where the best seal colonies can be found, when they have young and how to catch them. It is the most powerful fish in the ocean.

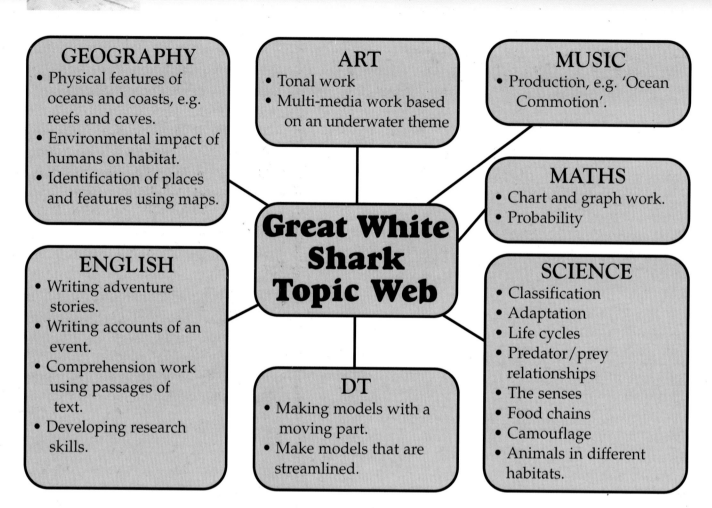

GEOGRAPHY
- Physical features of oceans and coasts, e.g. reefs and caves.
- Environmental impact of humans on habitat.
- Identification of places and features using maps.

ART
- Tonal work
- Multi-media work based on an underwater theme

MUSIC
- Production, e.g. 'Ocean Commotion'.

MATHS
- Chart and graph work.
- Probability

Great White Shark Topic Web

ENGLISH
- Writing adventure stories.
- Writing accounts of an event.
- Comprehension work using passages of text.
- Developing research skills.

DT
- Making models with a moving part.
- Make models that are streamlined.

SCIENCE
- Classification
- Adaptation
- Life cycles
- Predator/prey relationships
- The senses
- Food chains
- Camouflage
- Animals in different habitats.

Extension Activities

English
- Debate the issue of shark conservation.
- Write an account of a shark attack from the shark's point of view.
- Find and list collective names for groups of animals, or terms for their young, for example: pup.
- Write an article about sea life, using this and other books.

Science
- A shark's teeth are triangular: is this the most effective shape? Test others.
- Practical work and testing to find out how sound travels through water.
- Make food chains of other sea creatures.

Geography
- Look at the effects of pollution on the ocean habitat.
- Draw a map showing where great white sharks live in the world.

IT
- Use the internet to look at websites about sharks.

Art
- Work to develop a mural on the theme of conservation.

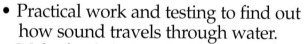

Glossary

Ampullae of Lorenzini Small pits on the shark's snout that pick up electric currents and help the shark find its food.

Blubber A thick layer of fat beneath the skin of an animal such as a seal. The blubber keeps the seal warm in cold water.

Cannibalism When an animal eats one of its own kind.

Camouflage A way of keeping out of sight by blending in with the surroundings.

Cartilage The elastic substance that makes up a shark's skeleton.

Claspers Special long fins that the male shark uses when mating.

Counter-shading Special patterns on an animal's skin that use light and dark colours to prevent it from being seen.

Courtship An animal's mating behaviour.

Denticles Tiny tooth-like scales on a shark's skin that protect it from getting scratched.

Embryo A young animal that has not yet been born.

Evolved Developed over millions of years.

Extinction No longer existing.

Fossilized Preserved by being turned into rock over millions of years.

Gills The parts of a fish's body that it uses to breathe.

Lateral line Special nerves and hairs along a fish's side that pick up sounds and movement in the water.

Paralyzes Prevents from moving.

Parasitic Surviving by feeding off another living thing.

Plankton Microscopic plants and animals.

Shoal A group of fish.

Tapetum A reflective layer in an animal's eye. Dogs and cats have tapetums, which is why their eyes glow in the dark.

Further Information

Organizations to Contact

WWF-UK
Panda House, Weyside Park,
Godalming, Surrey GU7 1XR
Tel: 01483 426444
Website: www.wwf-uk.org

The National Marine Aquarium
Rope Walk, Coxside, Plymouth,
Devon PL4 0LF
Tel 01752 600301
Website: www.national-aquarium.co.uk

The Shark Trust
36 Kingfisher Court,
Hambridge Road, Newbury,
Berkshire RG14 5SJ
Tel: (01635 551150)
E-mail:
sharktrust@naturebureau.co.uk

Websites

Sharks Homepage
www.oceanstar.com/shark
Information and tales about sharks, and links to other sites.

Books to Read

Great White Shark by Richard Ellis and John E McCosker (Harper Collins, 1991)

Sharks by M Oakley (Ladybird, 1995)

Sharks by Seymour Simon (Harper Collins, 1995)

Eyewitness Shark by Miranda MacQuitty (Dorling Kindersley, 1992)

Sharks by Niki Walker and Bobbie Kalman (Crabtree, 1997)

Index

Page numbers in **bold** refer to photographs or illustrations.